BEYOND HERE

With the compliments
of the Canada Council

Avec les hommages
du Conseil des Arts
du Canada

BEYOND HERE

Jim Green

thistledown press

Copyright © Jim Green, 1983

Canadian Cataloguing in Publication Data
Green, Jim.
  Beyond here

  Poems.
  ISBN 0-920066-68-2 (bound. — ISBN 0-920066-67-4 (pbk.)

  I. Title.
  PS8563.R43B4   C811'.54   C83-091064-6
  PR9199.3.G74B4

Book design by A.M. Forrie
Cover illustration by Jacqueline Forrie
Frontispiece drawing by Robert Hope

Typesetting by Apex Design Graphics Ltd., Saskatoon
Set in 11 point ITC Korinna

Printed and bound in Canada by
Hignell Printing Limited, Winnipeg

Thistledown Press
668 East Place
Saskatoon, Sask.
S7J 2Z5

This book is for
GRACE SKAVINSKI,
the fire of '77

ACKNOWLEDGEMENTS

Some of these poems have appeared in *Blackfish, Black Moss, Event, Inscape, NeWest Review,* and *Repository.*

"Lunch on the Fire Line" was originally published in Tom Wayman's anthology *A Government Job at Last* and "Elk on the Line" in his later anthology *Going For Coffee.*

Blackfish Press and Drednaught Publishing united their talents to produce "Morphine" as a beautiful broadside.

Special folks contributed to the creation of this book: Bart Robinson's counselling and guidance, Heidi Greco's editorial eye, and Allan Safarik's cleaving of the culls from the keepers.

Thank you friends.

My thanks to Canada Council Explorations for research and writing time and to the CBC for recording and airing some of these works.

This book has been published with the assistance of the Saskatchewan Arts Board and The Canada Council.

CONTENTS

Beyond Here 11
Awake 12
Coyote At Table 14
Quick Lunch 15
Raven Wind 16
Power Line To Sunshine 17
Saturday Chores 22
Bear On His Backside 23
The Day We Didn't Climb Cascade 24
Salad People 25
Yellow Flower 26
Elk On The Line 27
Fire Storm On Mount Whymper 28
What's A Little Secret? 34
Lunch On The Fire Line 35
Unaccustomed 36
Roughing It 37
Trout Feel Sexy 38
Canadian Pacific Moose 39
Dead Horse Winter 40
Drum Song 42
Morphine 46
Cameron River 48
Larch Valley Night Camp 49
Mount Assiniboine: Twenty-Six Trout
    And A Bottle of Teachers Scotch 50
Snap Shot 53

"Beyond" there lies, inwardly, the unconscious. Outwardly, the equipvalent of the unconscious is the wilderness; both of these terms meet, one step further on, as one.

— Gary Snyder

BEYOND HERE

Beyond here,
up a thousand feet,
on the third bench
above the valley
floor   there is an elk
carcass with grass
eight inches high
between the ribs,
and beside it a bear
skull with short
worn teeth and
no bottom jaws.

At night coyote
calls out from shadows
and dogs answer
back   talking tough,
bellowing to each other
how they'll rip
right out there,
raise hell
with a coyote or two
but   they never stray
beyond the fire light.

AWAKE

Awake   it's here
snow on Rundle's crest
cold wash skies

breakfast from fry pan
climb the north ridge
to sit and smoke

Who wants heaven? wrote Snyder
these words flooding my head
as Carl says
'You ever been to Portland?
Now there's a city you should see'

A bug   an insect I know
crawls across the pages
from *demonic wombs* to
deer don't want to die for me
then up a grass stem
and down again

I want her   heaven I mean

An Indian from Washington
freaked around like that bug
all winter in California
He roared his motorcycle
around the desert
'If I can't make it up one hill
I go back down and try another'
He wants heaven

These things flash
as I sit with spine to rock
on windwhipped ridge

and beside me
life-red pomegranate seeds
shrivel in the wind

aspen leaves
fall crisp
rustle

I want her
heaven
I mean

COYOTE AT TABLE

Nose in the chicken wire
up   down   round and round
till the hole's as big as his head
then tires of the job   leaves it
trots off without looking back
but sneaks around to hide
settles down for the wait
knowing it will work   always has.

Peering from green shadows
watching the hens find the hole
dive squawking into the coop
to come slowly clucking back
till one jumps up   checks around
then after a bit   hops down
on the outside   just in time
for lunch.

QUICK LUNCH

It was roosting on a limb
twenty feet off the trail.
My second rock nailed it.
Didn't even have a knife
but I tore the skin off
pierced belly with my nails
pulled the guts out
snapped the neck
broke off both legs
and the wings.
Fifteen minutes later
sitting by the ashes
sucking warm bones.
Spruce Grouse.

RAVEN WIND

Those ravens now

somersaulting

on the updraft

above the river

rising

dipping

rolling

playing catch

with a pine cone.

POWER LINE TO SUNSHINE

1

catch it
cup it in your hands
catch it
catch it while it rides
open wide the door
and in it slides

dry rustling aspen leaves
purring creek water sounds
dawn people
gliding in across the floor

sunrise
morning in the mountains
stars fading from the pink
splash of scarlet
dawn riders

2

stuff shirt in jeans
tug on boots
pull heavy wool sweater
warm around neck

jump down the steps
snugging on my hat
walking the aspen trail
to hot cakes and coffee

walking tall in riding boots
taking big strides
deep new day swells of air
smell of snow coming
leaves crunching underfoot
the sunrise   the sunrise
catch it

3

changes
    muffled fall morning
plump wet flakes
    spiralling
        down
           slowly
      earthward
   four full inches
of heavy fresh snow

climb in the truck
after second coffee
rattle up the road

4

stopping in on buffalo
see what they're up to
mornings like this
and can't find them
but are found ourselves
by coyote   nonchalant
trotting off into bush
dragging jack rabbit
from the side of his mouth

18

5

tush-splash   tush-splash
cow moose and calf
hooves suck popping from mud
dining on lily roots

calf lunging stilt-legged
out to deep water
both swim over
the other side

6

finally making it
the sunshine parking lot
hiking up the road
shovels and crow bars
moving mountains
planting forty foot trees
that have no roots
in the middle of the forest

the foreman pissed off
swearing about jackasses
being late for everything
except feeding and breeding

carl standing there
his head thrown back
mouth wide open
catching snow flakes
"world's biggest snow cone"
grinning
foreman grumbling
about "not being paid enough
to run no funny farm"

7

thirty foot pole
had to be sunk six feet
right where the chart says
on the bottom of a slide

we dug that hole three days
moved tons of rock
and the shale kept coming
we got a six foot hole
but she was ten foot wide

8

one last time
the foreman holds forth
about how we're finished
if we're late once more
not mentioning who else
would take the job
moving mountains in the snow

clattering down the road
warm in the truck cab

knuckle swollen   muscle worn
frump into soft chairs
cascade bar   beer

9

reading paper words
i almost missed the sunset
gold ribbed shimmering cloud
red streaked wolfberry leaves

solid   frozen peaks
cloud-shrouded all day
wrapped in last night's snow

pine needles glisten
the air cools
bugs fly by on stiff wings
bird calls soften

the sun dips
to limestone shoulders
pale light flashes bright
clouds turn pink   then grey
to musky haze
sawing wood rasps carry
as sounds become clear
and i didn't miss it

my back against a spruce
reading real words

SATURDAY CHORES

Both hands tightly
gripping the slop bucket
brim full
oh   so   carefully
living dangerously
on the flat deck
of the Diamond T

Afraid of it
like it was nitro
repelled by it but
almost hugging it
relaxed but on guard
as Carl drives
ever so slowly
up to the dump

Black bear woofs
scuttles to the aspens
puffing and grunting
when he gets a whiff
of our weekly deposit

BEAR ON HIS BACKSIDE

Up   side   down
legs splayed out   belly up
snout in the air,
undignified to be sure
but so is being trapped
in a fifty-two inch culvert
sprayed senseless
with a fly sprayer of ether
having your ass painted
yellow, trucked fifty miles
from your home ground,
turned loose on foreign turf
where every boar of the woods
knocks you on your tail
and sends you packing.

But that's the way it is
if they catch you at the dump,
around the new tourist camps
or down by the town site.
They set a trap for you
in your own back yard,
spray you to a pukey sleep,
paint your bum bright yellow
and truck you off to the bush
where you don't want to be
and if you dare to go back
one   two more times . . .

23

THE DAY WE DIDN'T CLIMB CASCADE

In a jumble of rock we found a path
Sheep trail, but no place for us.
What on earth are we doing here?
Fog banks lick at slick limestone.
We were drunk last night   how late?
Hung over, no food along, feeling sick
We descended to feast on raspberries.

SALAD PEOPLE

A visit to the garden
cucumber and green onion
tomato   sun warm
exploding   universal juices
around your mouth

Tiptoeing through melons
Banana Squash
Orange Orb
Turk's Turban
Eating crisp green beans
smelling dill
thumping pumpkin
palming corn cob

To the log house
cedar fire snapping
onion and garlic
mushroom in butter
soaring round the rafters

Pork chops smothered in mushrooms
zucchini snuggled in cheese
steaming mounds of brown rice
salad people from the garden

YELLOW FLOWER

The only thing today,
is praise   for a yellow flower
a dazzle   in a sun shaft.
Riding three days
my ass like two plums
rubbed raw in a knapsack,
stones poking through.
It's dark in this forest
has been for five miles,
the lathered horses
plodding the trail,
slumped in the saddle
      and there it is
this yellow flower
singing flower
proud flower
on a powerful
green stem
two feet high
in a brilliant splash
of sun lit grass.

ELK ON THE LINE

We had lots of help that trip —
about twenty mounted men
met at Windy Cabin, where
Snow Creek turns into Wigmore.

The plan was to push east,
sweep Panther Creek clean,
drive all the elk herds
clear across the Park Line
into the Province, to save
what little forage was left.

We lined out right across
the valley, high on the slope
both sides, started the drive.

All went well for a while
up past Sulphur Springs and
on towards the Forest Reserve.
We had a couple of hundred head
racing in loose bunches
wild-eyed   nostrils flared
hooves drumming the frozen turf
way out in front of the horses
till they saw the fence, bolted
south to the slopes of Dormer,
north towards Barrier Mountain.

FIRE STORM ON MOUNT WHYMPER

1

"Marble Canyon's going up;
if we don't get rain we're done for,
she'll rampage down the valley
clear to the Province."

Now that sounded serious
but hard to believe.
It meant the Bow Valley
would blaze up in smoke,
Banff, Canmore, and Exshaw
wither and succumb
and Calgary
burn down before the Stampede.

The sun burned
red through the smoke haze
above Banff Avenue.
Smoke crept around Rundle
to blanket Canmore.

It was west of Storm Mountain
where lightning struck an old snag,
small flames fermented and blossomed.
Fire ravaged the east side of Whymper,
was about to swallow Marble Canyon.
Cats were trucked fast to the fire line;
spotter planes, bombers, and choppers
were already backing the ground crews.

The cops knew how to get fire fighters.
Pulling up in front of the bar,
they waited for a while in the car;
then taking their time
and the volunteer roll,
they'd stroll right in
looking for customers.
Those that were left had excuses,
obligations, complications, and reasons,
or they would be only too happy, sir,
to stomp right out and do their duty.
The routine was not all in vain.
At the rear door was a touring bus
backed up tight to the wall
where two husky horsemen
were double arming the anxious
to a seat and a trip up the mountain.

In the morning,
waking up hung over and sickly,
rolling from gray blankets,
cursing the cold and their luck.
Red-eyed, stiff-backed, and big-headed,
squinting through the hot smoke,
blinking at the mountains of hose,
the stacks of axes and the shovels.

2

Hose over one shoulder
clenched tight in both fists
I'm dragging it uphill   upmountain
breath coming in hot rasps
sweat dripping into both eyes
my hard hat keeps slamming
whack   down onto my nose.

A mile and a half of canvas we need
to push water up from the river
one heavy duty pump   two relays
to reach the line.   Check grease
twist on the coupling   prime pump
yank starter rope   yank it again
again   it fires.   Water swells canvas
balloons the hose writhing upmountain
to the crew anxious in smoke.

Air choked with flying black needles
burnt crisp and feather light
flooding into mouth
filling nose and throat
or landing red hot
burning small crescents
on clothes.   Lungs
simmer till they hurt,
hot ground burns feet
eyes water
back is sore
legs are tired —
the pumps are all hammering
hoses swollen hard
there's water up there now
and   about bloody time
the truck with the chow.

3

We've strung hose along a new slash
half a mile   above the river
the fire's roaring in on two of us
standing there   waiting for water
holding the hoses limp
bug-eyed   scared as hell
ready to run from the flames.

A spotter plane darts in low
for once things work as they should:
a bomber dips in on target.
Water bomb slams towering fire wall
and we are lost
in a swirl of hot fog.
Then   in bops a chopper
and fearing the sticky pink mud
we are ready again to run
but smile to welcome the water
splashing heads and hot shoulders.

The hose twitches   goes stiff
water rushes the T-joint
gushes out my nozzle and his.
We turn the jets on each other
shower spray on upturned faces
soaking wet and screaming
laughing off the fear

4

The wind switched   blew back on the fire
it rained lightly that night
and steadily the next morning.
The line was held   pushed back
only a few spot fires left.

We'd manned that line the long night
flares winking red all around.
Dawn found us drained and hungry
so we quit for coffee and breakfast
some sleep in the morning light.

Sharpened sticks shoved in soft soil
draped with wet socks   shirts
steaming up-side-down boots
a strange cluster of totems
around a smoldering cook fire
in the burn above Tokumn Creek.
We were sprawled on our bellies
and backs near the fire
waiting for coffee to boil
dozing on the warm ground.

Camped by the loud creek
under black brush and spruce trunks
we didn't see it   or hear it
till too late
or too tired to care.
But it was far too late
when we scrambled wildly
dived for heavier cover
as the shadow bore down on us
jettisoned its load.

The chopper pilot was an ace
scored a dead center hit
blasted ashes into black faces
busted coffee pot and pack boards
scattered laundry and footgear
wiped out that camp fire for good.

WHAT'S A LITTLE SECRET?

A little secret is your very own;
like if you spread one hand wide
and wrap green toilet paper
round and round it
the way you usually do,
only this time you don't stop
and wrap on a great humungous ball —
just because you feel like it.

That's a little secret.

LUNCH ON THE FIRE LINE

Sitting on our hard hats
eating soggy sandwiches
in the drizzle
this Itallan guy
I'd been fighting fire beside
for three back busting days
tells me about the war

"It was rainy that day too . . ."
he says around a chunk of bread
going on to tell me
about pissing in the rain
in the mountains
and looking up to see a rifle
levelled at his head

He wasn't finished
so he kept pissing

When he looked up again
the enemy soldier
lowered the gun
tipped his helmet
and backed into the bush

UNACCUSTOMED

Unaccustomed
to receiving anything
that isn't typed up
blocked out
squared off
boxed in
in black and white
too many people
stand stiffly
in the shower
hearing the thunder
the drum of the water
with their ears
from the outside;
missing half the show
because ears work
from the inside too
so what you really hear
and truly feel
from the inside
is the driving rain
on your own roof.

ROUGHING IT

Carl was the one
who told me about her
told me what she said

They were roughing it, she said
across the bay at Fruitdale
splitting cedar to cook
lake water for drinking
light from kerosene lamps
a rock and gravel garden patch
with a clump of ancient apple trees.
No neighbours   not even radio
trying to make a go of it
and she'd hiked over   four miles
no   more like five miles
to borrow some rolling tobacco.

And she stayed   Carl said
six   no by God   seven days
ate about thirty gigantic meals
drank forty-seven gallons of tea
smoked two tins of Export Fine Cut
gulped down three green apples
that doubled her up right quick
and never the whole damn time
not even once   stopped talking.

They were roughing it, she said
that's what made her so lonely.

TROUT FEEL SEXY

Trout feel sexy
when they're spawning
in the clear gravel
beds of the stream
and they hide quick
when they see you,
stick their heads away
under the moss banks,
but if you're careful
you can reach under
caress their bellies,
work senuously up
to pulsating gills,
slide your fingers in.

CANADIAN PACIFIC MOOSE

Having climbed a hot day
blue sky with no wind
in the month of July
up to Hole-In-The-Wall
in the Sawback Range
we sat in the cool
shadows of the damp cave
before a wild scramble
down the water course.

Hot   that was the day
and sweaty   smelly sweaty
when we hit the bottom
spied the slow backwater
of the Bow River inviting,
stripped our clothes
beside the railway line,
dove deep to dark water
cold but feeling so good
we burst to the surface
blowing   and whooping.

Too cold to stay in long
we swam to the grade
were about to climb out
up the rounded bank
when hair pulled loose
filling both my fists —
moose in the water
courtesy of the C.P.R.

DEAD HORSE WINTER

He made it back to the ranch
in two long days   snow piled
three feet when he left town,
covered the top wires
by dawn next morning
as he leap-frogged along
with two worn-out horses
lunging at chest deep drifts.

The cattle were bawling
bunched up in the creek bed.
He sucked them out with the smell
of loose hay and a trail
punched through by Clydesdales
dragging the sled.   He set out
next day for the horses
but his mounts bogged down
just short of the ridge.
He jammed his saddle in a tree
sent the horses on the backtrail
and floundered on alone
with snowshoes made of aspen,
strips from a grey blanket
and strings from the saddle.

The last days were the worst,
searching the still canyons
for stranded   wasted bands,
the killing   blood
splattered dark on crystal white,
the numbing slam of the rifle
and the screams.
The lucky ones were dead
already   the rest almost gone,
slumped walleyed in soft snow
just slack hide and hard bones,
they had no tails left and
even manes were missing where
they'd chewed on each other.
Sticks poked through
slashed cheeks   gums raw
bloodied from crushing branches,
the last of the feed.
He shot and kept shooting,
killed a hundred and more
first with a long gun
till he ran out of shells,
finished the last of them off
with an old Savage shotgun.

In the spring   a gelding
with eight gaunt mares in tow
came down from the valley.

DRUM SONG

bum bum bum bum bum bum bum bum bum bum bum
bum bum bum bum bum bum bum bum bum bum bum
bum bum bum bum bum bum bum bum bum bum bum
bum bum bum bum bum bum bum bum bum bum bum
The drums   the drums   the beat of the drums
the beat of the drums   the beat of the heart
the beat of the heart   the throb of the land
the throb of the land   the throb of life
the throb of life in the beat of the drums
the power   the power   the beat of the drums
the drums   the heart   the land   the life
the power in the heart of the drums of life
the drums   the drums   the beat of the drums

I'm sitting on dried grass facing the water
bum bum bum bum bum bum bum bum bum bum bum
the sun is sinking behind the black islands
bum bum bum bum bum bum bum bum bum bum bum
a raven stiff wings by to its nightly roost
bum bum bum bum bum bum bum bum bum bum bum
an end of the day loon call rings clear
bum bum bum bum bum bum bum bum bum bum bum
Women soft step the log dock with tin pails
bum bum bum bum bum bum bum bum bum bum bum
bend to crack the skim ice with their heels
bum bum bum bum bum bum bum bum bum bum bum
scoop up cold water for empty tea kettles
bum bum bum bum bum bum bum bum bum bum bum
and a kid runs by pushing a small red wagon
bum bum bum bum bum bum bum bum bum bum bum
a load of water in a green plastic barrel
bum bum bum bum bum bum bum bum bum bum bum

42

Behind me   the throb   the beat of the drums
the beat of the drums   the throb of life
the throb of the drums   the beat of death
the beat   of death

bum bum bum bum bum bum bum bum bum bum bum
bum bum bum bum bum bum bum bum bum bum bum
bum bum bum bum bum bum bum bum bum bum bum
bum bum bum bum bum bum bum bum bum bum bum

The old lady knew she was going to die
had them fly her back to the settlement
beside the clear lake where she was born
Word was sent out to the other villages
people arrived by boat   plane   and canoe

They came   shook her hand   said farewell
to the tired grey lady of ninety years
grandmother to half the town
come home to die

She smiled to see her friends once more
listen to the waves slap the sand shore
the sharp fall wind in the swaying pine

She died Wednesday
everyone gathered at the small log house
clasping her still hand   a final touch
drinking tea and quietly playing checkers
Planes came Thursday and more the next day

The burial by the lake was Friday
with preparations for the feast underway
they burned her clothes on the beach
a blaze of dry willows on the sand

Hung her thin mocassins in a tall pine
sung hymns in the wind-blown cemetery
cooking pots   bubbling in every house

In the evening the people came together
the visitors   relatives   and the kids
carrying pots   buckets   and tea kettles
The young men served for the feast
kept serving till there was no more
plates piled high with fresh roast caribou
steaming white fish   trout   warm bannock
apples   oranges   jam   butter   lard
a bowl of blood soup   canned peaches
and gallon after gallon of tea
Almost an hour to share all the food
enough to last everyone there for days

Then came the speeches
old men remembering yesterday
talking about today   about death
about the land   about life   about tomorrow
After the feast   the drums   the dancing
together   round and round the log hall
the swaying circles pulsing to the drums
through the night   into the morning

That was yesterday   today
the drums are going strong again
as I sit near the still lake shore
only there is a difference today
The drums speak another language
as the skins are heated for the hand game

a hand game   a game of power
a game of power   a game of life
a gambling game   a game of money
a game of skill   a game of power
a game of the drum   a game of life

Getting up from the brittle grass
I walk down to the drum house
where the teams have been picked
the drum skins warmed up
and the chants are rising
the game has begun
I step into the drum thunder

It is a new beat   a sound of the heart
the beat of the heart   the sound of life
the throb of life in the beat of the drums
the power in the heart of the drums of life
the drums   the drums   the beat of the drums
the beat   of life

kaBUM kaBUM kaBUM kaBUM kaBUM kaBUM kaBUM
kaBUM kaBUM kaBUM kaBUM kaBUM kaBUM kaBUM
kaBUM kaBUM kaBUM kaBUM kaBUM kaBUM kaBUM
kaBUM kaBUM kaBUM kaBUM kaBUM kaBUM kaBUM

MORPHINE

Pale blue walls of the surgery ward
become plunging waterfalls and erupting fountains
the browns and yellows of the window curtains
swirl to crimson flames and spinning pinwheels
in a fluid display of phosphorescent fireworks

Remembering back to that first night's blur
blood bubbles from my arm into little bottles
"take a deep breath hold it"   X-ray zap
urine sample   stool sample   "how old are ya?"
intravenous long plastic needle up left wrist
all night riding the bed pans
pan after pan after pan   never falling off one
just riding them as they come all night long
shit all over the place
but too wasted to give a damn

Then lying there a day and a night and a day
bottle after bottle of the clear juice dripping
    down
    into
    my
    left
    arm
Gradually it's good to be lying there feeling better
the days settle in and it's a good life

A fine early morning breakfast
followed by a hot bath   some days a shower
read for a while till the Doc shows
shoot the breeze with him
lunch time
afternoon nap   and some slow reading
till supper hour
shuffle through a poem or two
watch a couple of hours of tv
then to bed for a backrub
from a big-busted Scottish nurse
and drift into sleep   knowing
things have gotta change

It's too bad because it's nice to just sift along
but there's danger there
so without a purpose
but feeling I should have one
I pick another direction
and there are no waterfalls here

CAMERON RIVER

Paddling back upstream
long   slow strokes
taking deep full breaths
reaching for the calmness
the lucid fluid thought
that comes with integrating
the merging elements
of a complex movement.

Back-paddle in a wide arc
the current catches the bow
canoe side-slips backwards
slowly turning
to come full around
picking up speed
plunging downstream
to the pitching rapids.

Jay stroke   hard
straighten her out
follow the water pull
ride the crest
left of the flat rock
right of the shallow trough
hold there
slide into it . . .

Overhead pass
stretch to side-paddle
back over   dig deep
pull   canoe bow drops
way down   tosses high
slices through the curl
darts past the boulders

Knees weak   arms aquiver
heart thumping   brain racing
peering down river.

LARCH VALLEY NIGHT CAMP

High on the mountain it's cold.
The clouds creep among the rocks
Slip between us around the fire
Where we sit drinking sweet wine
In the silent rainweeping fog.
So here we are, wet at 7500 feet
Waiting for the skies to clear
Hoping to climb Temple at dawn.

MOUNT ASSINIBOINE: TWENTY-SIX TROUT
AND A BOTTLE OF TEACHERS SCOTCH
(Kodak message for Garry Kozak)

Assiniboine wasn't actually in the photograph.
Your hat was.   It was lying on the grass to the
right with a wilted yellow blossom in the band.
There was an over-turned galvanized pail in the
left background.   You could see the rusty holes in
the bottom. A half bottle of Teachers Scotch was
plunked on the boards about in the middle
of everything.   There were four boards, two feet
long, nailed together by slats across the back.
The boards were grey and cracked and had that
fuzzy surface that came off on your hands when
you rubbed them.   Old boards.   Once a shutter
on one of the Alpine Club cabins.   The Scotch was
sitting on that.   The trout were laid out in a row
on the old shutter, then spilled out in double
rows over the short grass.   There were twenty-six trout.

It's a fine color shot.   Trout fresh from the lake,
a good looking stetson and a bottle of Scotch.
Grey, weathered boards, an old bucket and the green
brown fall grass.   You have to stand up and step
back to see the mountain.

Back up six feet, turn slightly to the right, and
let your eyes rove slowly upward.   Above the pines,
the talus, the cliff face, and the ice.   Way up . . .
and there it is . . . Mount Assiniboine   all 11,870
feet of her.   The peak radiant, fresh with the
night's snow; glistening.   Cold.   Blue and white
and black frozen rock.   The wind tearing away
at the new snow, pluming it off to shower
the Gloria Lake basin.

But we're down below warming our hands on the
breakfast fire. A crisp morning   clean, sharp
air. We're feeling good, feeling alive.   And we
are happy too, that yesterday is past.   Remembering
how hot it was when we hefted our
packs at the mouth of the Spray and headed west
up Bryant Creek.   How tired and sticky we were
by the time we trudged past Gibraltar Rock,
the sun sagging lower and lower but all of us
determined to make it over the pass.   How dark
it had become by the time we made Cascade Rock.
Cave Mountain looming up black to the bright
stars.   And still we kept on, half-way up
Assiniboine Pass, stumbling in the dark, till
it suddenly hit us that there was no need (that
and fatigue)   unrolled the bags and slept by
the trail till first light.   Made the camp in a
little over an hour.   The sun was climbing
through Wonder Pass as we bounded over the
meadow and jumped the creek.   Assiniboine and
her double, the sister reflected up-side-down
in the blue of Magog Lake.

Flap-jacks and fried eggs.   Ham hot from the pan.
Steaming coffee   hands cupped warm around the
mugs.

It wasn't a fishing trip.   With extra equipment
from Monod's, the plan was to climb the Horn.
Mount Assiniboine by the north west ridge.   Up
from the lake on the skree to the first cliff.
Traverse the glacier westward to the ridge and
then on up.   Sounds simple.   It wasn't and it
isn't.   It felt good to all of us that it didn't
have to be done.   It was there all right, but
obliterated by flying clouds   blizzards of snow
and ice, lashed by hurricane winds.   Save for a
few moments that first morning we never saw
the top half at all.

I found a bird's nest of old fishing line by
that little brook running into Gog Lake.
Crawled the gravel for half an hour and finally
discovered a number twelve snelled hook, leader
and all.   Speared a piece of wool from my
sweater, let it float with the current to the
lake.   About eight feet out   blip   it ducked
under.   The line zig-zagging across the water.
It happened again, and again.

You were cleaning your trout below camp in the
rollicking waters of Magog Creek.   I charged off
down there to your bellering, nearly fell in
laughing to find you thrashing around waist deep
in the ice water.   Seemed your gutted catch had
taken life, slithered from a pool to the stream,
and were slipping off down country.   We found
most of them and before they lit out again, laid
them out with the others   took the picture.

SNAP SHOT

Hey   here's one of me
on my trusty steed
left hand full of rein leather
right firmly gripping the halter rope
of a stocky little pack horse
looking back over her left shoulder.
My stetson has my face shaded
but you can see my beard
and just the right amount of boot toe
sticking out the stirups
and the way I . . . . . .